THE
Archive Photographs
SERIES

BRENTFORD

Brentford High Street, looking east from the Market Place early this century. It was narrow, very busy and notorious for its traffic jams.

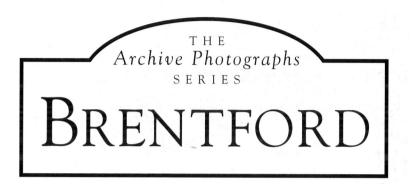

THE
Archive Photographs
SERIES

BRENTFORD

Compiled by
Carolyn and Peter Hammond

CHALFORD

First published 1996
Copyright © Carolyn and Peter Hammond, 1996

The Chalford Publishing Company
St Mary's Mill, Chalford,
Stroud, Gloucestershire, GL6 8NX

ISBN 0 7524 0627 2

Typesetting and origination by
The Chalford Publishing Company
Printed in Great Britain by
Redwood Books, Trowbridge

Cover picture: Brentford Market porters in the 1950s.
(Courtesy of the Brentford and Chiswick Times*)*

ON THE CANAL,
BRENTFORD.

(COPYRIGHT PHOTO)
WAKEFIELD, BRENTFORD

A peaceful scene on the canal near Clitherow's Lock, Boston Manor. The canal played an important role in the commercial life of Brentford from its opening in 1794 until the middle of the twentieth century.

Contents

The drinking fountain in the centre of the approach to Kew Bridge photographed in 1893. A gift from the Metropolitan Drinking Fountain and Cattle Troughs Association, it was unveiled by the Duchess of Teck in July 1877. It was removed to Western International Market in 1974, but gave its name to the Fountain Leisure Centre.

Introduction

Brentford is an old and historic town. It has existed from at least the Roman period, if not earlier, on the main route from London to the west at a point where the River Thames and the River Brent could be forded and later, crossed by bridges. Traces of a Roman road have been found in excavations just north of the present line of the High Street. For a large part of its history it was technically divided into Old and New Brentford, to the east and west respectively, although this division must never have been very obvious to those passing through.

It grew in importance through the Middle Ages as the traffic on the road out of London increased. As its importance as a staging post became apparent, coaching inns such as the Star and Garter at Kew Bridge, and the Castle, the Three Pigeons and the Red Lion further along the High Street, were established to provide refreshment and extensive stabling for travellers. The fertile soil encouraged the growth of market gardening and this, together with industries such as boat building, brewing, brick-making and tile-making meant that from a very early time, the town grew in size and importance. Thus when the canal was built in 1794 the town was well placed to take advantage of the increased commercial activity that this encouraged. In the nineteenth century it grew relatively fast, although this was not entirely to its advantage. As commercial activity grew with the addition of soap works, breweries, a tannery and then an ever-expanding gas works, the town acquired a reputation for being a rather smelly, dirty place, with considerable overcrowding and slums. The High Street in particular, was notorious amongst travellers for its narrowness and traffic jams. Market gardeners selling their produce straight from their carts parked along Kew Bridge Road did nothing to help this situation which did not improve until the local authority was forced to provide proper market premises in 1893.

Much was done in the second half of the nineteenth century to improve the public amenities in Brentford. Civic pride saw to it that the imposing Vestry Hall, swimming baths, library and fire station were built, as well as several new churches. Many of these improvements were overseen by the Local Board, later the Urban District Council, which was led by Thomas Layton, a well known local worthy who bequeathed his collection of books and antiquities to the town. The Council's Architect and Surveyor, Nowell Parr, designed many of the public buildings illustrated in this book before going into a private practice specialising in public houses.

In the latter part of the nineteenth century attempts were made to improve some of the worst slum housing but there were still many small alleyways left in existence at the beginning of this century. The High Street was widened in parts when trams were introduced, although this seemed, in many ways, to make the jams worse. House building continued, particularly after the Great West Road, built in 1925 to by-pass the jams in Brentford, brought more jobs to the area in the new factories which soon grew up along its length.

The second half of the twentieth century has seen great changes: the decline of the old industries, the closure of the docks and the gas works, the proliferation of office blocks in place of shops and factories. Post-war redevelopment has swept away many of the streets of small terraced houses and the High Street has changed almost beyond recognition. Fortunately we still have photographs of the town as it was. Some were taken by anonymous photographers but many came from the well-known firm of Wakefield, which had a shop in the High Street and which was ever alert to an opportunity to produce a good postcard. Others were taken by the architect and tram enthusiast S.G. Jackman, to whom we owe some splendid High Street scenes from the 1930s. Some interesting shots come from the *Brentford and Chiswick Times* which celebrated its centenary in 1995. We also owe a debt of gratitude to Fred Turner, who wrote the standard history of Brentford and ran the public library for forty one years: he collected photographs of the area and himself recorded many events and picturesque scenes in the life of the town at the end of the last century and the beginning of the present one.

The photographs in this book have been arranged as a tour of the town in six sections, starting at Brentford Market then proceeding westwards along Kew Bridge Road and the High Street to the bridge over the canal. We have made detours up side turnings as we came to them as well as a sortie through the Market Place and into the Butts. We then travelled up the Half Acre and Boston Manor Road, followed by a look at the River Thames, the docks and the canal and finally went along the Great West Road to Gunnersbury Park.

We hope that we have produced a record of Brentford in the recent past that will help to both awaken, and keep alive, an interest in Brentford's history and heritage.

Acknowledgements

We acknowledge our indebtedness to all those who have written on the history of Brentford before us, and in addition our thanks go to the following who shared their expertise in various subjects with us while we were researching the captions: Val Bott, Andrea Cameron, Neil Chippendale, Richard Clarke, Gillian Clegg, Barry Collis, Nadine Dunn-Meynell, Sonia Harrison, Janet McNamara, Ruth Maranzi, James Marshall, Cyril Smeeton, Diana Willment, James Wisdom, Elizabeth Wood and Colin Woodward.

The majority of the photographs in this book have been taken from material in the collections at Chiswick Public Library and Gunnersbury Park Museum, and we thank the London Borough of Hounslow Leisure Services Department for allowing us to use them. In some cases these were copied from originals held by other institutions or individuals and we would like to thank the following for permission to reproduce their photographs: *Brentford and Chiswick Times*: 13, 25a, 42, 63b, 104, 106, 115b, 120; Gazette Newspapers: 12b, 14a, 27a; John Gillham: 57b; executors of the late S.G. Jackman: 26a, 49b, 52, 75b, 116; Marples Construction Limited: 96; National Motor Museum, Beaulieu: 107b, 122; Mr and Mrs Pearce: 39; Royal Botanic Gardens, Kew: 121b; Mrs Emily Stafford: 49a, 63a; Ian Stratford: 17.

We are most grateful to the following for allowing us to borrow items from their collections of postcards: Mrs Mary Brown: 12a, 34b, 44, 47b, 51, 61b, 81b, 89a, 91b, 92a, 97, 102a, 105b; Douglas Cotterell: 11b, 16b, 38a, 46b, 53a, 61a, 64a, 65b, 80, 95a, 101b, 102b; Peter Downes: 36, 41b, 53b, 57a, 67b, 69b, 72, 100a, 109a, 117b; and James Pearce: 117a.

One

Brentford Market to Ealing Road

In its heyday Brentford Market covered all the land on the north side of the main road now occupied by the Fountain Leisure Centre and the office blocks and warehouses of Capital Interchange Way. It provided an outlet for selling the produce of the many market gardens in the vicinity of Brentford. Together with the other three large local employers: the Grand Junction Waterworks, the gas works and the Royal Brewery, it dominated this part of Old Brentford.

A mid-nineteenth-century oil painting of London Stile Farm. This was a large farm and market garden which stretched from Green Dragon Lane to Gunnersbury Avenue. Brentford fruit and vegetable market was built on part of its land.

Laying the foundation stone for Brentford market in January 1893. This enclosed market, which included covered sheds around the sides for perishable goods, shops along the High Road frontage and paved areas for stalls and waggons, replaced the informal market which had been held around the fountain at Kew Bridge until congestion there forced a move. This market played an important part in the economy of the area, providing an outlet for the produce grown in the local market gardens and nurseries.

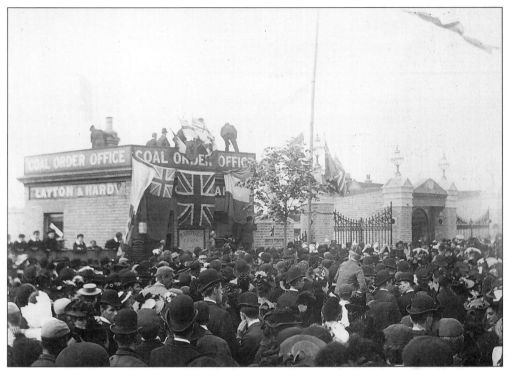

The crowds gathered outside the gates to see Alderman Knill, the Lord Mayor of London, officially open the new market on 24 May 1893. The be-flagged coal office was that of Layton and Hardy, local coal merchants and both prominent in local affairs.

A view of the front of Brentford market, showing the shops along the High Road frontage, taken in the early 1920s.

This card was posted in 1946, but the lorries, loaded with bananas, date from at least twenty years earlier than that. Newman's had been in the market since at least 1900.

The well-known entrance to the market extension photographed in 1970, just four years before the market was renamed Western International and moved to Southall. The 1893 market building was so successful that more space was soon needed and a large extension was built in 1905 to the design of Nowell Parr, Architect and Surveyor to Brentford Urban District Council.

Three vegetable porters, working for a firm called Shillaker, in the 1950s. Left to right they are: Arthur Basley, George Cheney and Mike Clarke. The sacks of potatoes they were carrying weighed 112 lbs (more than 50 kg).

A market porter, 'Mac' MacCarthy, who worked in the 1950s for a firm called Greenwoods, who dealt mainly in fruit and vegetables. He is seen here carrying baskets of mushrooms and pot plants.

The interior of the market in 1929. The sides of the extension built in 1905 can be seen on the right.

Kew Bridge station, designed by Sir William Tite and built in 1849, is seen here in the 1850s. The railway is the London and South Western line from Waterloo to Hounslow. In the background is the Grand Junction Waterworks Company's pumping station. The tall, iron lattice standpipe was built to maintain even water pressure in about 1852; it suffered serious frost damage in January 1867 and was rebuilt within a protective brick tower later that year.

Kew Bridge approach, taken after 1903, when the third Kew Bridge had been built. The Star and Garter Hotel, an eighteenth-century coaching inn, is on the right and on the left can be seen the Express public house.

A 1920s advertising card overprinted for Brentnall & Cleland, a local coal merchant. Their coal yard was in Lionel Road, conveniently close to the railway line. On the back of the card is an advertisement for the coal that could be supplied – the best, 'B & C's Inland House Coal' cost 52/6 (£2.63) per ton.

The Express, erected in the 1860s, opposite Kew Bridge. In the doorway can be seen the licensee, Mr Kerlich, which dates the photograph to 1879. Oddly, this public house did not serve the beers brewed locally, but those from a firm in Bishop's Stortford, which had a depot at St Pancras Station. Robert George Aldington took over the pub in 1882 and the family have been there ever since. According to a poem written earlier this century, from the Express and the Star and Garter at Kew Bridge, to the Coach and Horses at Brentford End, Brentford could provide fifty pubs for the delectation of drinkers.

The toll house and gates at Kew Bridge in about 1870. The bridge was freed from tolls on 8 February 1873 by the Lord Mayor of London, the gates ceremonially removed and taken away on a dray belonging to the neighbouring Royal Brewery.

The approach to Kew Bridge after the removal of the toll gates. Not long after this picture was taken the bridge was demolished because the steep gradients were a danger to traffic and it was no longer wide enough. This was the second bridge on this site, built in 1789 to replace a timber brdige which only lasted for thirty years.

The second Kew Bridge photographed in 1898, just before it was demolished, showing through the arches the temporary wooden bridge that replaced it while the new bridge was being built. The pumping station tower can be seen in the background.

Kew Bridge in the course of demolition in 1898.

The tram terminus at Kew Bridge. The electric trams came to this point in 1901 and later that year the line was extended along Brentford High Street to Hounslow. This picture comes from a self-congratulatory book produced in 1901 by the operators, London United Tramways, as a souvenir of the introduction of the service. In the background can be seen the Prince's Hall, opened in about 1890 as a hall and beer garden.

Outside the Star and Garter hotel on Charter Day, 18 October 1932, part of the celebrations to mark Brentford and Chiswick being raised from urban district to borough status. Here the Lord Lieutenant of Middlesex, Lord Rochdale, is greeted by the Charter Mayor, James Clements JP.

The Prince's Hall, whose entrance gate is seen in the picture opposite, became in turn a swimming pool, roller skating rink, dance hall, cinema and film studio until rescued from dereliction by Jack de Leon, who turned it into the successful Q Theatre. Under his management it ran from 1924 until 1956. It was closed and also demolished in 1957. The site is now occupied by the Ralph M. Parsons office block.

Kew Bridge Road, looking west, photographed in 1891. Market produce is being sold from the carts parked along the sides of the road; the congestion this caused led to demands for a properly organised market and the subsequent building of the covered market in 1893.

Kew Bridge Road looking west in about 1910, with what appears to be a steam car on the extreme left outside the Grand Junction Waterworks, which has now become the Kew Bridge Steam Museum.

The Salutation Inn, at the turn of the century. It was on the north side of the High Street, just west of the waterworks. It closed in about 1920 and the site is now a petrol station.

PUBLIC CAUTION.

Brentford Gas Company.

WHEREAS

JOHN LEEDON and **GEORGE CHAMBERS** have been convicted of Breaking One of the Company's **LAMPS**, placed by the Side of the Road at *HAMMERSMITH*, and not having paid the Penalty awarded against them, were *committed to the HOUSE of CORRECTION for the Space of*

ONE MONTH!

The Company give this Notice, that Offenders may know the Punishment they are liable to.

By Order of the Board,

BRENTFORD,

14th *April,* 1823.

☞ Printed by W. GLINDON, Rupert Street, Haymarket.

THOˢ. JULLION, Clerk.

Vandalism in 1823! The Brentford Gas Company was founded in 1820 by Felix Booth, owner of the Royal Brewery. At first the gas was only used for street lighting, but after the 1840s it was available for daytime domestic use as well.

Brentford Gas Works from the river in 1926 at the start of its expansion onto the site formerly occupied by the Royal Brewery. The shutes on the left are to allow the barges to be loaded at high tide.

The gas works in 1958. It was eventually closed in 1963.

The 'Coke Gang' at the gas works in about 1920. They worked on the coke ovens for thirty shillings (£1.50) per week.

Looking back towards Kew Bridge Road in May 1935. On the left in the mid-distance is St George's church, with the gas works' buildings looming on either side of the road. At its largest the works covered $8\frac{1}{2}$ acres on both sides of the High Street and used 600 tons of coal per day.

The south west end of Distillery Road in April 1964, looking towards the High Street, at the overwhelming bulk of the gas works. Two years later the demolition of the road began – to be replaced by Distillery Walk.

The gas cooling plant in the 1950s.

The memorial to the gas works employees who died in the First World War, unveiled on 9 July 1922. This used to be on the wall of the works situated on the south side of the High Street, opposite the little school building. The milestone has long since disappeared.

St George's, the first church in Old Brentford, built by the Trimmer family and other subscribers in the 1760s as an unconsecrated chapel and consecrated as a church in 1828. This photograph was probably taken shortly before it was demolished in 1886.

The rather plain interior of the first St George's church in the 1880s. The high pulpit obscures the altar piece of the Last Supper, painted by Johann Zoffany who used local people as models for the disciples. The painting now hangs in St Paul's church.

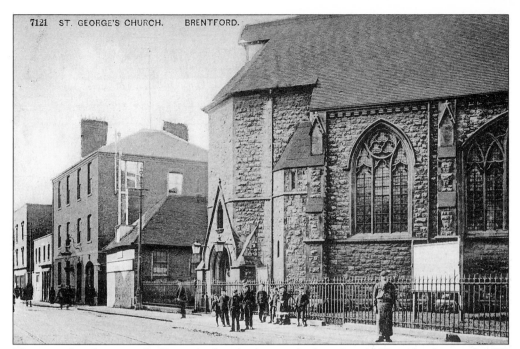

The second and current St George's church as it was built in late 1887 to the design of A.W. Blomfield, but without a tower.

St George's with the tower added in 1913. This was partially paid for from the £1,000 left for a peal of bells by a parishioner, Thomas Layton, previously the chairman of Brentford Local Board and later of Brentford Urban District Council. It was originally intended that the tower should be surmounted by a spire but this was never built.

The interior of the new St George's, decorated for Christmas, before the First World War. It was closed as a parish church in 1959 and has been used as a museum for mechanical musical instruments since 1963.

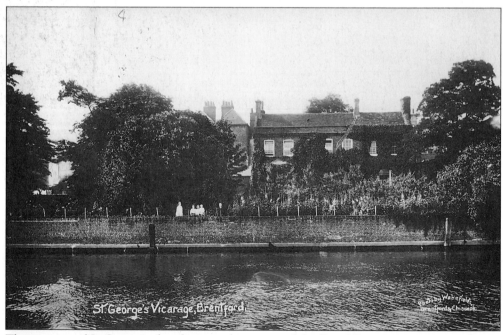

The vicarage of St George's church situated just west of the Royal Brewery, approximately one hundred yards away from the church on the river side. It was demolished in about 1931 as part of the expansion of the gas works. This card was produced as a Christmas card from the vicar, the Revd Thomas Selby Henrey. It shows the family immortalised in the book *The King of Brentford* in their garden.

A Brentford pottery *c.* 1850 from a contemporary naive painting. At that date it was run by George Robinson, whose name can be seen on one of the chimney pots. Its premises were north of the High Street at the top of Pottery Road. It closed down just before the First World War. The availability of suitable clay soil led to the growth of a number of potteries and brick and tile kilns in the eighteenth and nineteenth centuries. Most of the clay pits have been filled in and built over, but the Potomac Pond in Gunnersbury Park is said to be the site of an old pottery.

A trade card produced for the Royal Brewery early in this century, showing the imposing brewery building and the adjoining Brewery Tap public house, refronted after 1900. The firm was called the Red Lion Brewery until 1829 when King William IV allowed the name to be changed in commemoration of his visit there to discuss polar exploration with Sir Felix Booth. On the back of this card is a pro-forma order form for Royal Stout and Light Bitter Ale, which was especially brewed to supply the 'family trade'.

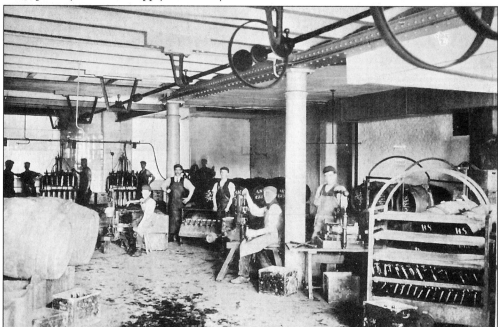

The yard of the Royal Brewery in the early 1920s. Brewing ceased here in 1923 and the works were demolished in about 1926 when the gas works expanded onto their site.

The bottling stores in the Royal Brewery in the early 1920s. These included cold storage to keep the beer in as good condition as possible until delivery.

One of the Royal Brewery's pubs, the Albany Arms, at the corner of Albany Place c. 1910 when the licensee, seen here, was Mr Frederick Coles.

Brentford High Street at the junction with Ealing Road in the 1950s. On the corner of Ealing Road is the old Red Lion public house, built in 1905 and demolished in 1965, when it was replaced by a modern pub with the same name on the opposite corner.

A local shop at No.1 Market Terrace, Albany Road, photographed in 1915 judging by the news placard headlines.

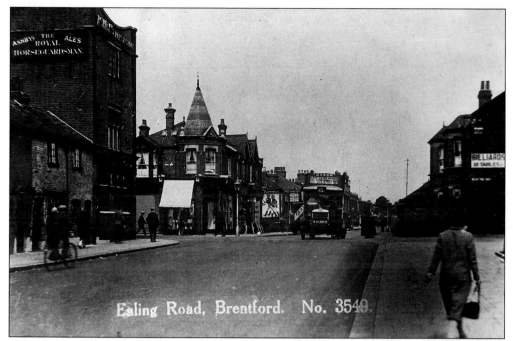

Ealing Road at the junction of Albany Road and Walnut Tree Road, looking north, in the early 1930s. There was a billiard hall on the corner of Walnut Tree Road.

The Brentford Football Club team in 1932-33, whose ground, Griffin Park, is further up Ealing Road. This was a very good year for the club as they won no less than three cups. Jimmy Bain their captain is in the centre, on the left of their chairman, L.P. Simon.

IN LOVING MEMORY OF

BRENTFORD

WHO FELL
FIGHTING FOR THE CUP.

Bravely we stepped on the football field,
The honour of our town to uphold,
But we were playing foemen who would
 not yield,
And in the finish they had us stone cold.

And now they are heading for Wembly's
 trail,
A wonderful team no doubt,
And if they play only half as well,
They will knock the best of them out.

PEACE, PERFECT PEACE.

A postcard produced in 1927 to commemorate a less successful year when the Brentford team lost to Reading in the fifth round of the FA cup.

A gale on the night of 31 December 1904 caused much damage in Brentford, including blowing off the roof of the main stand at Griffin Park

Two

The High Street

Until the building boom in the second half of the nineteenth century Brentford High Street was in a sense the town itself, a jumble of shops, houses and workshops, with the larger industrial premises sandwiched between the High Street and the river. It was intersected by narrow alleyways and yards of small cottages and tenements. It had a reputation for being dirty, smelly and a bottleneck for traffic. The coming of the trams led to some road widening and slum clearance but it is the postwar redevelopment that has changed it almost beyond recognition.

Osbornes' Dairy, a typical shop at No.315 High Street in about 1902. Among other things the dairy also sold confectionery. The price of the milk and the number of deliveries per day are worth noting. The Albany Parade shops now occupy this site.

Brentford Police Station at No.42 High Street. This building was erected in 1869, replacing the first police station on the corner of Town Meadow Road. It was vacated in 1966 when the present police station in the Half Acre was opened and pulled down in 1969. This police station is said to have been the one used in the credits for the BBC TV series *Dixon of Dock Green*. The site, opposite Charlton House, is now occupied by an empty office block.

A photograph of the staff of the police station to commemorate the coronation of King George V in 1911. The sergeants are in the front row, the constables in the back, with Inspector Schofield in the centre. The officers with sabres were mounted policemen.

King Edward VII, a converted 42 foot launch, rigged to scale as a 10 gun brig, on its way to the royal family's lake at Virginia Water in 1904. Converted at Sheerness and towed up the Thames to Brentford to be taken to Windsor by road, she is seen here being pulled by a splendid steam traction engine in the High Street outside No.279, Field Body and Sons, Wheelwrights, opposite the fire station.

The building known as the Cage in 1897 just before it was pulled down and the fire station erected in its place. It was used as a place of detention for criminals before their appearance in front of the magistrates.

The fire station, built in 1897 to the designs of the Brentford District Council's architect Nowell Parr, to the latest specifications, with a 'commodious engine room' to accommodate two appliances, a hose tower for drying the leather hoses, recreation and watch rooms and a yard for drilling. It was closed as a fire station in 1965 and is now used as offices.

The funeral of a fireman killed on duty *c.* 1910. The procession, with the firemen in the brass helmets they wore for ceremonial occasions, is in the High Street near the fire station.

Looking eastwards towards the fire station before the First World War. On the left can be seen the traditional striped barber's pole of Horton's Barbers shop.

Rattenbury's shop was a well known landmark in the High Street, selling new goods at No.288 and running a pawnbroking business from No.289. It closed in January 1968 and the shop fronts were removed to a Museum of London store later that year for preservation. This photograph was taken in about 1958. The shop site is just to the west of the Albany Parade car park.

Horton's Barbers shop at No.276, seen previously, and here shown in about 1908. Messrs Horton seem to have been versatile, since as well as cutting hair they did much else, including re-covering umbrellas and sunshades.

R. Ashley, General Grocer, at No.263, opposite the Rising Sun in about 1905. They are selling ham rolls at 2d (1p) and sandwiches – an early example of a take-away food shop. This site is now the grounds of Berkeley House.

Brentford Conservative Club Rowing Club in 1913 after a successful season. They are sitting in the garden of the Conservative Club, on the north side of the High Road at No.264, opposite Town Meadow Road and Pump Alley.

The Rising Sun public house, No.68 on the south side of the High Street, in the early 1900s, next to a building with a poster proclaiming proudly that it was soon to be the site of an Electric Theatre. This was never built as far as is known; the first cinema in Brentford was the short-lived Electric Empire in the Market Place. On the right of the picture is Pump Alley.

Low lying parts of Brentford were always prone to flooding. In 1906 this picture was taken in Town Meadow Road, into which Pump Alley leads.

This shop in the High Street also appears to be suffering from flooding, with a fire brigade hand-drawn steam-pump apparently pumping out their basement. The firemen are wearing their work-a-day flat caps, not their splendid brass helmets. Lodge, the scale makers were on the north side of the High Street, opposite Pump Alley.

MECHANICS' INSTITUTION,

FOR BRENTFORD AND THE VICINITY.

TWO LECTURES
ON

ELOCUTION

WILL BE DELIVERED BY

MR. G. C. DAVENPORT,

(Late Editor of the Bury and Suffolk Farmers' Journal)

AT THE BRITISH SCHOOL ROOM, OLD BRENTFORD.

LECTURE I.
On Tuesday Evening, March 11, 1845,

The following portions of this interesting subject will be considered and explained ;—
ARTICULATION and PRONUNCIATION.—Formation of the Voice.—The Pure Sound of the Vowels, &c.— Distinctness.—Effect. INFLEXION and MODULATION.—Interrogation.—Supplication.—Exclamation.— Parenthesis. Illustrated by "The Passing Bell."—Hood's "Number One," and several other Sentimental and Humorous Extracts.

LECTURE II.
On Wednesday Evening, March 12, 1845,

The following will be explained :—
INFLEXION and MODULATION, continued.—Pitch of Voice in Speaking or Reading, and its extent.— Intervals.—Management of the Voice.—Speaking or Reading Voice.—Expression.—Time.—Passion—its modulation. Prolepsis, or Anticipation.—Communication.—Satire.—Climax.—GESTURE. Illustrated by Extracts from Shakspeare.—Burns.—Hood.—Byron.—Joe Miller, &c. &c.

The Lectures will commence at 7 o'Clock. Members will be admitted on presenting their Tickets, and each Member may introduce a Lady.

☞ A single Ticket of Admission, for Non-Subscribers, may be had for ONE SHILLING ; and a Ticket to admit Two Persons for Eighteen-pence: and they may be procured of Messrs. NORBURY and Mr. MURPHY, or of the SECRETARIES. Schools will be admitted on payment of Sixpence for each Person.

J. FIGG,
W. WHITMAN, } *Hon. Secretaries.*

The Victorian enthusiasm for self improvement took many forms. These lectures were held in the British School building in Old Spring Gardens, where the school was founded in 1834.

The British School moved to a new site in the High Street in the 1850s. Later it was renamed the Rothschild School after its major benefactors, the Rothschild family of Gunnersbury Park. It was closed in 1930 when Brentford Senior School, in Clifden Road, off Boston Manor Road, was opened, later to become Brentford Girls School. The British School building was demolished in 1936 and replaced by the health centre.

7119 BRITISH SCHOOLS.   BRENTFORD.

Form One in the British School in 1925. Miss Smith the teacher is at the back on the left; the headmaster, Captain Revell, is on the right. The school was strictly segregated: girls on the ground floor and boys on the first floor.

These two boys are Horace and William Devenish, twins who attended the British School in the early years of this century. In 1912 they were awarded five pounds by Leopold Rothschild for completing seven year's perfect school attendance. They had obviously also won many other prizes.

A scene in the Brentford Town Mission Hall in Old Spring Gardens on 5 March 1914. At the back are the carcasses of sheep, part of a consignment sent from Australia to the Ragged School Union for distribution to the poor of London. Brentford's share consisted of five sheep, plus one more bought with donations from local philanthropists. In the front are the families selected to receive the joints. Frederick Marriner, a local butcher and his son helped cut up the carcasses. Old Spring Gardens was on the east side of the present County Court site.

Brentford was well known for its
many narrow alleyways. This is New
Spring Gardens in the 1950s which
disappeared in the early 1960s when
the new county court was built on
the site.

The High Street in May 1935, looking east towards the gas works. New Spring Gardens is on
the left, next to the Brentford Tyre Service at No. 246.

An early postcard view of St Paul's church, just north of the High Street at the top of St Paul's Road. Built in 1867/8 to serve the west part of Old Brentford, it became the principal church of the United Parish of Brentford in 1961. It was imaginatively reconstructed in 1990/2, providing a meeting area in the former nave, and a new area for worship on the north side.

The interior of St Paul's church in 1896.

S. Paul's Vicarage. Brentford.—

St Paul's vicarage, just north of the church, showing the vicar Robert Dand and his family in the garden in the mid-1920s. This area is now part of the grounds of Brentford School for Girls.

St Paul's recreation ground before the First World War. The Local Board bought the land for a recreation ground with money raised to celebrate Queen Victoria's jubilee in 1887, but due to various problems the ground was not opened until 1889.

The High Street, looking east, in May 1935, not long before the trams were superseded by trolleybuses. The cross-over which allowed the trams to switch from one track to the other to avoid obstacles is visible in the foreground.

The Beehive Hotel, with its familiar beehive on top, at the corner of the Half Acre around the time of the First World War. When the Half Acre was widened for the introduction of the tram service the pub, rebuilt to a design by Nowell Parr, became the corner property, having previously been two buildings away from it. On the back of this card we learn that at this time luncheons were served daily, from 12.30 until 2.30; the 'Ordinary', the fixed price lunch, cost 1/4d (7p).

The corner of Half Acre and the High Street before the First World War. Goddard's furniture store is now on the site of the bank; the shops to the left of the bank were demolished around 1968. The crowd here are apparently waiting for something to happen.

The north side of the High Street in July 1905, giving a closer view of the shops in the previous picture. There is a dustcart outside Tarrants; the dustmen had to climb up the ladder at the side to tip in the rubbish.

Bradbury's wholesale grocers shop at No.108 High Street founded c. 1860. The entrance to their yard can be seen on the right, in the centre of their ninety foot frontage. These buildings have long since gone, but their premises were approximately where Lloyd Brennand are today.

Workmen in Bradbury's yard loading onto one of their vans a consignment of sugar from Henry Tate and Sons – who did not become Tate and Lyle until 1921. This scene probably dates from about 1905, when Bradbury's had a fleet of twenty horse-drawn vans delivering groceries to shops within a radius of twenty miles.

Henry Band's tannery in Old Plough Yard between No.115 and No.114 High Street. Band's was one of those firms which probably did as much as any to add to the rich cocktail of Brentford smells. Here the men are removing the skins from pits of lime and water, where they have been soaking, ready to scrape off the fur, fat and flesh.

Another process at Band's tannery whereby hair and fat were removed from the skins which were then stretched on frames to dry, in the background.

An advertising postcard produced in about 1910 by Poole's butchers shop, opposite Bradbury's, at No. 204 High Street. Standards of hygiene were obviously not so important then, particularly considering how near the shops were to the road, with horses and carts continually passing by.

The High Street in June 1966, looking east from near the Market Place towards the Half Acre. The old shops are being replaced by a modern shopping parade. The recently completed post office can be seen on the extreme left.

The north side of the High Street in about 1908, looking westwards near the Market Place. The Three Pigeons and the Red Lion were both old coaching inns with extensive stabling to cater for travellers. The Three Pigeons was used by the magistrates until 1850, when the town hall was built. Most of the male figures are in uniform so it is possible that the horse-drawn dray is part of a military convoy from Hounslow Barracks.

The High Street in 1905, looking eastwards in front of the Market Place. It was very narrow and a notorious traffic bottleneck. This card was posted in Brentford at 5.15 pm to tell the recipient, also in Brentford, that its sender would not be back in time for tea.

The site of the Three Pigeons just after demolition in the late 1950s. This is now the site of a tile shop.

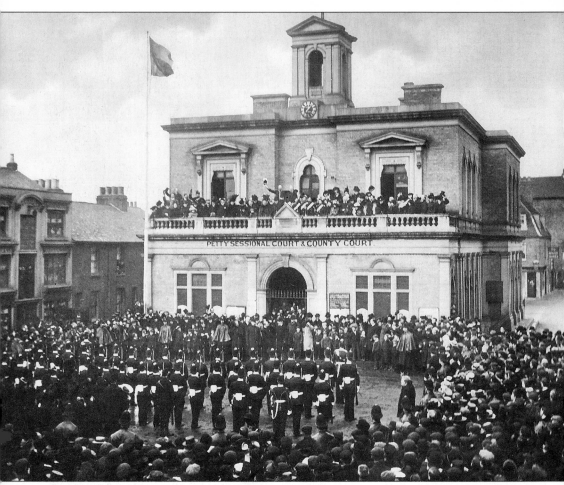

The High Sheriff of Middlesex reads the public proclamation of Edward VII as King from the balcony of the Town Hall on 28 January 1901. This building was erected in 1850 by the Brentford Town Hall and Market Company who leased rooms for the county and magistrates courts and to other official bodies as well as for public meetings and social events. In 1891 it was bought by the Middlesex County Council and became a full-time court house.

The weekly market in full swing in front of the town hall in 1906. This had been held here since the fourteenth century. It was closed in 1933. In the background is the old post office built in 1886, which moved to St Paul's Road in 1908.

The staff outside the post office in the Market Place in 1904. They are wearing their typical 'fore and aft' caps and include a row of small telegraph boys in front.

Brentford Fair in front of the town hall in 1893. It was established in the fourteenth century and held here for three days in May and September until it was abolished in 1932. Behind the swing boats on the left can be seen the living waggons of the show people.

A scene from the parliamentary election of 1880, when last minute voters were rushed to the hustings set up in The Butts. Herbert Gladstone, younger son of W.E. Gladstone, Prime Minister that year for the second time, was standing against Lord George Hamilton and Otavius Coope for the Conservatives – who won. The results were proclaimed from the town hall balcony.

The town hall at the end of the Second World War, with an anti-blast wall built in front. The building was renovated in 1929-31 and given a new front.

Metal being poured into moulds at George Spicer's works by Messrs E. Martin, D. Bartier and R. Hibury in 1957. Spicers were an old family firm who made marine propellers. Their premises can be seen on the east side of the Market Place in the picture above and had originally been the post office. It was swept away in the redevelopment of the early 1960s.

Behind the town hall, seen here in the centre at the back, is The Butts, an enclave of late-seventeenth and early-eighteenth century houses. This photograph was taken in about 1920 and the lack of cars is noticeable.

Charles Smith, a local chimney sweep, in The Butts, c. 1910. His bundle of rods can be seen on the back of his cart. Smith lived in Windmill Road for many years, as did his son William, who followed his father's trade.

Brentford Cottage Hospital early this century. A dispensary had been opened in the High Street in 1818 and then transferred to this building on the corner in The Butts (now Nos.24 and 26) in 1893, where there were also six beds for in-patients and a base for the nurses working in the community.

The front of the new hospital which opened in Boston Manor Road opposite the railway station in 1928. This was closed in 1977 and became an old people's home. It was recently demolished and doctors' surgeries and other health care facilities are being built on the site.

McIlroy's drapers shop in the High Street, about 1900. The building still survives, but is now Motorwise, a car hire and repair firm.

An accident outside McIlroy's. This is one of the postcards produced by Wakefield, the local photographer whose shop was just down the road from here. He must have been very quick off the mark!

The High Street in 1905 looking east, showing Wakefield's shop at No.137. Gas lamps on brackets over the shop-fronts were very common at that time. Wakefield's was next door to the vicarage and is now an empty site.

Another traffic jam in the High Street. The problems must have increased after the trams arrived. Two trams side by side (the double tracks can be seen here) must have taken up nearly all of the available space. Mr Wakefield, who produced this postcard, obviously felt strongly about this!

Noy's House, the home of Sir William Noy, attorney general to King Charles I and buried in St Lawrence's church, was a Brentford landmark in the last century. It was next to the old St Lawrence's vicarage. Noy's House was probably a Tudor building. This picture was taken not long before both were pulled down in 1889.

The south side of the High Street to the west of St Lawrence's, whose fifteenth century tower, the oldest building in Brentford, can be seen in the background. This was taken not long before the trams came in 1901. The carter in the foreground is carrying Fuller's beer, not beer from one of the local breweries. It is probably being delivered to the Six Bells public house which was a Fullers pub.

The interior of St Lawrence's church, early
this century and probably decorated for
harvest festival. The church was closed for
worship in 1961 but is still standing.

St LAWRENCES CHURCH BRENTFORD.

ST. LAWRENCE'S CHURCH & VICARAGE.   (View from Wakefield's.)

Photo by WAKEFIELD, BRENTFORD

A postcard showing the south side of St Lawrence's church and the vicarage, taken by
Wakefield the photographer from his back garden. A large and obviously hand-drawn flag
appears on the church tower – this is occasionally seen on Wakefield's postcards.

The entrance to Durham Wharf, between No.171 and No.170 High Street, leading down to the canal basin photographed in 1961. The trams have long been replaced by trolley buses, as can be seen from the overhead cables. This area has recently been cleared for redevelopment.

Another of Brentford's alleyways. This one is Percy Cottages, St Lawrence's Place, just east of Durham Wharf. This photograph was taken during the Second World War.

An accident before the First World War, near Durham Wharf. The cart was carrying used straw from stables as manure for local market gardens. The fact that Christmas greetings are printed on the back of such a card seems rather odd to us today.

The High Street looking east from Brentford Bridge. This picture was taken in 1904, judging by the jubilee sign over Pennington's shop, a well-known outfitters, who celebtated their centenary in 1954, but closed in the 1960s.

King Edward VII being driven over Brentford Bridge in about 1905. Oddly enough none of the bystanders on the bridge seem to be very interested. By then Mr Wakefield was calling himself an 'automobile photographer'.

A romantic view of one of the more exciting events in the history of Brentford, the Battle of Brentford, November 1642, painted by John Hassall in 1928 for the local MP, Col. Grant Morden. The parliamentarians were trying to prevent the Royalists advancing on London but were overwhelmed and the Royalist forces sacked the town.

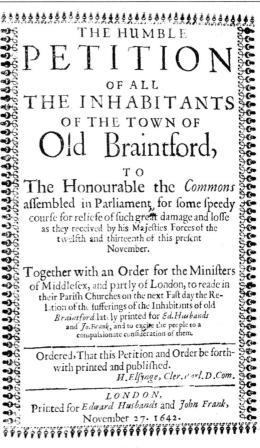

THE HUMBLE

PETITION

OF ALL

THE INHABITANTS

OF THE TOWN OF

Old Braintford,

TO

The Honourable the *Commons* assembled in Parliament, for some speedy course for reliefe of such great damage and losse as they received by his Majesties Forces of the twelfth and thirteenth of this present November.

Together with an Order for the Ministers of Middlesex, and partly of London, to reade in their Parish Churches on the next Fast day the Relation of the sufferings of the Inhabitants of old *Braintford* lately printed for *Ed. Husbands* and *Jo. Frank*, and to excite the people to a compassionate consideration of them.

Ordered, That this Petition and Order be forthwith printed and published.
H. Elsynge, Cler. Parl. D.Com.

LONDON,
Printed for *Edward Husbands* and *John Frank,*
November 27. 1642.

The front page of the petition sent to Parliament asking for help after the town was sacked; most of the parishes in and around London contributed to a relief fund.

Brentford Bridge photographed from the west shortly after it was widened in 1909. It is at least the fourth bridge on this site and was built in 1824 to replace an earlier brick and stone structure.

An auto train at the 'up' platform of Brentford GWR station, looking towards the docks. The Great Western Railway opened a spur line from Southall to Brentford Docks in 1859. The passenger service ceased in 1942 and the station was demolished in 1957. Freight trains still used the line until the docks closed in 1964.

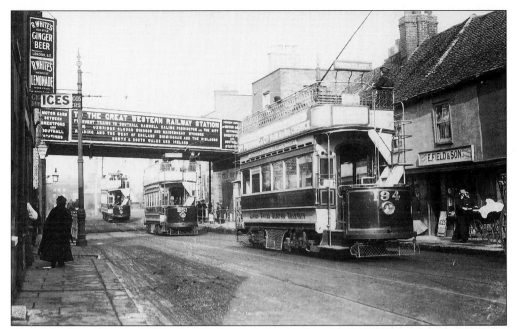

Trams passing under the railway bridge carrying the spur line of the GWR to Brentford docks in about 1913. They are travelling towards Brentford although they are on the wrong side of the road; crossovers allowed the trams to switch from one set of tracks to the other to avoid obstructions.

The same scene in 1935. The railway bridge was demolished in 1966. The entrance to the railway station is on the left. It was described in 1866 as 'impractical for ladies in rainy or windy weather'.

Syon Park House, on the north side of the road west of the railway bridge, photographed at the turn of the century. A century earlier it had been a school at which the poet Shelley had spent two unhappy years. The house was demolished in 1953 and the site is now the Royal Mail delivery office.

Three
Half Acre and Boston Manor Road

The turning off Brentford High Street called the Half Acre leads into Boston Manor Road (known as Boston Road until 1933) after a short distance. It was always a major route to Boston Manor and Hanwell, and formed the boundary between Old Brentford to the east and New Brentford, the smaller western part of the area. Much of the surrounding land belonged to the Clitherow family, the owners of the manor until the 1920s.

A tram at the terminus in the Half Acre soon after the service to Hanwell was introduced in 1906. The conductor is transferring the trolley pole to the Hanwell-bound wire for the return trip; the cross-over to allow the tram to move onto the left hand track is just visible beyond the tram.

The east corner of the High Street and Half Acre in 1904 before it was widened for the introduction of the tram service. On the corner is a butchers shop which was at one time run by Frederick Marriner who helped cut up the free lamb donated to the poor of Brentford. (see page 48)

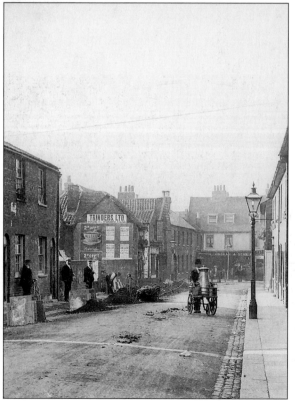

Milk delivery in the Half Acre in 1905; work is starting on the road widening project. The junction with the High Street can be seen in the distance.

The Half Acre, looking towards the High Street, with the Vestry Hall on the left. This photograph was taken before 1905 when the old buildings on the left were demolished for road widening.

Road works in Half Acre in preparation for the tram lines, showing the same buildings as the picture above but from the other direction.

The 'proposed new Vestry Hall', built in 1899, shown here in the drawing by the architect, Nowell Parr. The building fronted onto the Half Acre, on the corner with St Paul's Road. The shops on the right were never built. The building included a large hall seating 600 with a stage, two committee rooms, offices for the collectors of the poor rate and a soup kitchen in the basement. In 1907 the county court moved here from the town hall and remained until the new court building in Alexandra Road was opened in 1963, when the Vestry Hall was demolished. The police station now stands on the site.

An early view of the post office in St Paul's Road, nearly on the corner with Half Acre. It moved here from the Market Place in 1908 and closed in 1960 when the new post office opened in the High Street. The site is now a car park.

The Congregational church in Boston Manor Road in about 1910. It was built in 1783. After bomb damage in 1944 it was restored with reduced accommodation when it apparently lost a storey. The congregation joined with the Presbyterians to form Brentford United Reformed church in 1972 and then with the Baptists to become Brentford Free Church in 1994.

Congregational Church, Brentford.

Clifden House at the junction of Boston Manor Road and Windmill Road in the 1920s. It was built for the Viscount Clifden in about 1730. The Urban District Council and its predecessor, the Local Board, had their offices here from 1888 until the amalgamation with Chiswick in 1927. Next to it, on the right, can be seen the Public Library which was erected in 1904.

The Clifden House hall and stairway, taken just before their demolition in 1953. The old signs at the foot of the stairs to 'Rate Collectors Office, Council Chamber, Conservative Association' tell of its former use.

The first Brentford Urban District Council, and some of their officers, elected in 1894. Those we have met elsewhere in this book are: Thomas Layton the Chairman, a well known local worthy and antiquarian (seated in the centre), Nowell Parr, their architect (standing second from the left at the back) and James Clements who was to be the Charter Mayor in 1932 (seated on a cushion front right).

Clifden House also housed the public library from 1890 to 1904, although it is apparent from this photograph of the reading room that they were in need of larger premises to fit in all the books, magazines and pictures! The 'Silence' notice in the background was typical of libraries at that time.

This picture shows the back view of Clifden House in 1903: on the left is the area of its garden where the new public library was soon to be erected. Photographed by Fred Turner the librarian, in keen anticipation of his new library!

Brentford Public Library, opened 9 May 1904. It was designed by Nowell Parr, the Council's architect, and paid for by a gift of £5,400 from the American philanthropist Andrew Carnegie, who attended the opening ceremony. Fred Turner the librarian is standing proudly in the doorway. He was appointed in 1889 to inaugurate a library service for Brentford and continued to run the library until his retirement in 1930.

Laying the foundation stone of Brentford Baths, in Clifden Road, just off Boston Manor Road, in 1895. Holding the trowel is James Bigwood, then MP for the Brentford Division of Middlesex. On his left, holding the trowel's presentation box is Thomas Layton, Chairman of the Council and on his right, with his hand proprietorially on the stone is Nowell Parr, the Council's architect who had designed the baths. As well as the swimming pool there were to be ten slipper baths for men and five for women, as well as a wash house and laundry.

The main pool under construction in 1896. In the winter the pool could be floored over and the resulting hall used for social and other events.

Brentford Baths, photographed soon after they were opened in 1896. The sexes were originally strictly segregated: the left hand door for 'Men' and the right hand one for 'Women'. The tall chimney of the boiler house can be seen on the left.

Clifden Corner, Brentford

We live about 2 minutes walk from here. This is the public library

The corner of Boston Manor Road and Windmill Road, showing Clifden House and the Wesleyan Methodist church. This was built in 1889 and the spire added in 1903. In 1964 it was demolished and replaced by a block of flats, called Clifden House, with a smaller church next door.

WINDMILL ROAD BRENTFORD

Looking up Windmill Road, before the First World War. On the right is the Methodist church.

The station house at Brentford in 1906. The station opened in 1849 on the London and South Western Railway line from Hounslow to Waterloo. The figure in the gateway is probably the station master Mr Alfred George Teakle.

One of two volunteer service companies of the Middlesex Regiment entraining for the Boer War at Brentford station in 1900. There is a memorial on the wall over the staircase in Brentford Library to the local men who lost their lives in that campaign.

Brentford station in 1910 with a passenger train entering the station going to Waterloo. The station house is on the left. There were about the same number of trains to Waterloo then as there are now, but the cost (slightly later, in 1923, as we could not find the figures for 1910) was 1/2d (6p) for a third class return fare to Waterloo.

The station in 1895 photographed from the Windmill Road bridge. The products of a local pottery are stacked in the goods yard on the right.

The Boston Manor Road entrance to Beldam's Packing and Rubber Company premises photographed in the 1960s. Next door is Prospect House an eighteenth-century building, now used as offices, under the shadow of the elevated part of the M4 motorway.

Two of Beldam's lorries in the 1920s. The firm was founded in Windmill Road in 1897 as the Beldam Foundry and became a rubber factory in 1911. They finally left Brentford in 1988.

Boston Manor Road in the early 1900s before the tram lines were laid for the route to Hanwell 1905/6. Boston Farm, demolished in 1928, is in the background. The photographer is photographed: Mr Wakefield is caught on film while setting up his camera beside his car, which has his familiar logo on the back. Traffic was obviously light.

Boston Manor Road looking north, just north of Boston House, ie the same view as in the postcard above, but about thirty years later.

Boston Park Road in the early 1900s. The Roman Catholic church, opened in 1866, can be seen in the distance on the left.

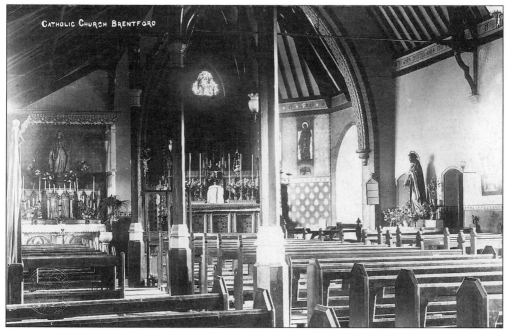

The interior of the Roman Catholic church, in the 1920s.

The entrance gates to Boston House in Boston Manor Road in 1918. This and the next picture come from the sale catalogue when the estate was first put on the market.

Boston House from the drive in 1918. It was built in 1622 and extended in 1670, when it was bought by James Clitherow. It remained in the Clitherow family until bought by Brentford Urban District Council in 1923. The grounds were opened as a public park in 1924.

In the grounds at Boston House in the early 1900s, when it was owned by the Clitherows. The postcard was apparently sent by one of the staff who has written on the back 'this is our kitchen… these are my fancy boys, two gardeners and a footman'.

The seventeenth-century state drawing room at Boston House in 1911, photographed by Fred Turner. This part of the house is open to the public on Saturday and Sunday afternoons from spring to autumn.

The elevated section of the M4 under construction in October 1964. The long span of the motorway goes over the rooftops of what was originally the Macleans factory (mid-left) and subsequently Rank Audio Visual, before crossing the park. Boston House can be seen among the trees top right.

Four

River, Docks
and Canal

Waterborne traffic brought by the Thames, the River Brent and later by the Grand Union Canal, was one of the main reasons for the growth and importance of Brentford as a centre of commerce. The decline of this trade generally parelleled the commercial decline of the town.

A view of the Brentford river front just west of Kew Bridge, probably taken in the 1960s. The Brentford Timber Company, just behind the Waggon and Horses pub, had been there since the 1920s. The large brick building, now derelict, was a training centre for telephone engineers, built about 1964. It is arguably more attractive from the back than from the front.

Beating the bounds, an ancient ceremony to mark the boundaries of a parish, was still carried on in Brentford up to the 1920s. Here the elders and choir boys of the parish of Old Brentford are taking full advantage of the possibilities offered by the river boundary. This photograph of 1911 shows the official party on *Fury*, a steam tug owned by James Clements, Charter Mayor in 1932, of Clements Knowling & Company.

Beating the bounds in 1925, one of the last times the ceremony was carried out. This time those beating the land boundaries use a charabanc.

A scene on the ice during the Arctic winter conditions in 1891 when the Thames between the bank and Brentford Ait froze over. At one time in February of that year the temperature fell to 4°F (-15.6°C). In this view from The Hollows, the men look as if they may have come from the shops in the High Street.

The Bunch of Grapes, at the bottom of Ferry Lane, in about 1907. For many centuries a ferry operated from here to Kew. The public house was built about 1880. Later known as the Ferry Hotel it was demolished in 1983.

The ferry in 1939, just before it ceased operation, with the last ferryman Mr Charlie Humphries.

The Brentford Monument, photographed by Fred Turner in 1909 soon after it had been erected on the wharf at the foot of Ferry Lane. It commemorated four events in the history of Brentford and was made from columns of granite discarded from Brentford Bridge when it was widened that year – an early example of recycling. It is now outside the County Court where it was moved in 1992.

On the west side of Ferry Lane was the Thames Soap Works of T. B. Rowe, shown here in about 1904. The firm had moved to Brentford in 1799 and remained on this site until 1933, when they were removed to Silvertown by Lever Brothers who had become a major partner in the firm in 1916.

Jupp's Wharf and Granaries in about 1905, a short way up river from the Brentford monument and from T.B Rowe. Originally they were maltsters, taking advantage like many other firms, of Brentford's grain trade. The two Thames sailing barges at the wharf are particularly interesting.

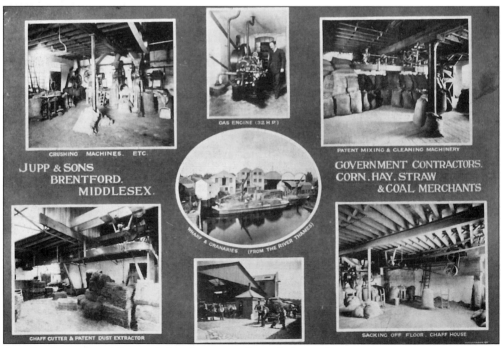

Another Jupp advertising card showing scenes from their warehouses.

A Clements Knowling motor tug, the *Ceekay*, in the late 1950s, in front of the massive GWR dock warehouse. After a merger with another firm the boat was sold in 1967.

Brentford Docks in 1928 in a view across the basin towards the GWR warehouse seen in the picture above. The dock buildings had been built to designs by Isambard Kingdom Brunel in 1859, but had been rebuilt after a disastrous fire in 1923.

Brentford Docks in 1957. At that time more than fifty barges a day passed through on their way up the Grand Union Canal to the north or down river taking cargoes to load onto vessels at London Docks. Timber and coal were important cargoes, as well as manufactured goods.

Coal being loaded onto barges at the docks in 1923. From here coal, arriving by train on the GWR branch from Southall, was sent for export or for use in places situated on the river.

Coal wagons being unloaded in Brentford Docks before the First World War.

A barge wedged under Brentford Bridge during a high spring tide in the 1960s. Many of the goods being shipped into and out of the docks came via the Grand Union Canal. Here one such shipment misjudged the state of the tide and had to wait three hours before continuing its journey.

Brentford lock basin showing how busy it was when in full use, in this case in 1906. In the background is the gauging lock in its second (double) form, built after the original, single lock, had been washed away in a flood in 1898.

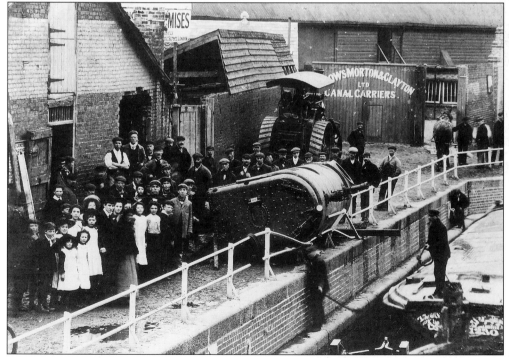

An accident on the the canal bank early this century beside the railings that can be seen on the left of the picture above. The boiler was presumably being taken into or out of the confectionery factory on the left when it capsized, nearly ending up in the river.

The gauging lock at Brentford after a record rain fall in June 1903.

The old water mill which backed onto the Butts, in about 1900. The mill was demolished in 1904 when the Boatmen's Institute was built.

The Boatmen's Institute, built to a design by Nowell Parr for the London City Mission in 1904. It aimed to provide basic education, religious instruction and also a maternity room for the boat people. It is now a private house.

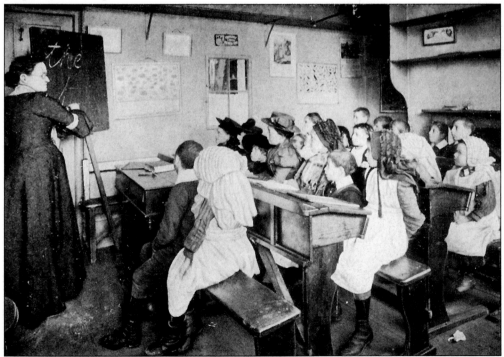

The schoolroom of the Boatmen's Institute soon after it opened. One of its aims was to help educate the children of the boatmen during the brief periods when their family boat had stopped to load or unload cargo. The little girls in the foreground are wearing their traditional bonnets.

Mathilda Styles, the youngest daughter of a canal boat family early this century. She is dressed in her working clothes and holding a windlass for operating lock gates.

Two young girls in traditional costume on their boat, photographed in 1893.

Five

The Great West Road

The Great West Road was built in the 1920s to provide a fast, new route to the west. Starting east of the town, it joined the Staines Road at East Bedfont, bypassing the notorious bottleneck of Brentford High Street. Modern factories were attracted to the area in the 1930s by the good communications and ready availability of land, and at the height of its prosperity it was known as the 'golden mile'.

The road under construction in the early 1920s. The houses on the north side of Adelaide Road can be seen on the left, but the south side of the road has gone: one of the few areas where houses had to be demolished. The gardens of the adjacent York Road are on the right.

King George V and Queen Mary driving along the Great West Road in the royal limousine to attend the opening ceremony on 30 May 1925. An unbroken stream of bunting decorated the new road from Kew Bridge to Syon Hill and cheering crowds lined the route. The local people treated it as a public holiday.

King George V cutting the tape to open the road. The ceremony was performed in front of a grandstand decorated in blue and gold which was set up just west of the Boston Manor Road junction.

The Great West Road from the GWR railway bridge looking towards Boston Manor Road in the distance, in 1925, soon after the road was opened. The absence of road markings at this date meant that motorists could, and did, drive all over the road.

Part of the procession celebrating Charter Day, 18 October 1932 (see also page 21). This car is carrying the representatives of the Brentford and Chiswick Chambers of Commerce to the ceremony. The Chairman of the Chiswick Chamber, Mr Hedley Fry, is wearing his chain of office.

Another float in the Charter Day ceremonies. This is one of the carts belonging to the Council's Works and Highways Department.

Queen Mary visiting the new Coty factory which opened in 1932. Very soon after the road opened, many large firms took advantage of the speedy new transport links with London and the west. As a result some splendid factories were built along its length.

Two of the staff in Coty's cosmetic department in 1957. At this date they were producing over seventy thousand lipsticks every week.

The Great West Road at the junction with Boston Manor Road in August 1935, probably photographed on a Sunday as the modern Feltham type trams were normally used on the busy Uxbridge to Shepherds Bush route on weekdays. This view looks south to Park Baptist church, known as the 'church in the fields' due to the open fields of the area in 1855 when it was constructed; it was demolished in 1990. The little box on a column in the foreground is a call point for the fire service.

Macleans Corner, Great West Road, Brentford.

The north west side of the same road junction as on the opposite page showing Macleans' factory. It was probably taken soon after the factory opened in 1932. The building was later taken over by Rank Audio Visual and sadly, now stands empty.

Sperry Gyroscope Company's factory from an advertising postcard printed soon after the factory was opened in 1931. The layout ,with its architecturally striking administrative blocks set in landscaped grounds designed to hide large areas of standard factory buildings behind, was typical of most of the new premises built along the road. Here they manufactured navigation systems for aircraft, ships and weapons.

Carville Hall, photographed in 1962. This was originally known as Clayponds Farm. The estate was bought by the Middlesex County Council in 1918 and the parts not required for building the Great West Road were bought by Brentford Urban District Council in 1922 with some of the money raised for a war memorial (the rest of the money was used for the memorial in front of Brentford Library). The estate was opened to the public as a recreation ground the following year.

Looking westwards along the Great West Road March 1962. In the centre is the Smiths Crisps factory and on the left, the Martini Tower, burnt down in May 1989 and rebuilt by Data General who now occupy this site. Smiths moved to Kew in 1970 and their buildings were demolished in 1988.

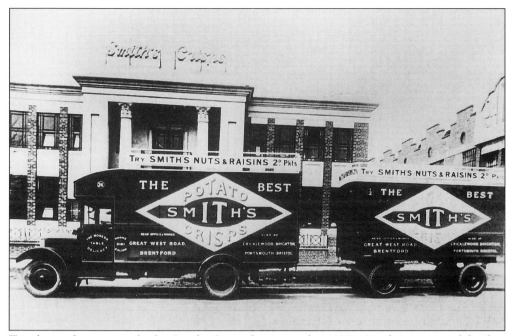

Two liveried vans outside the Smiths Crisps factory in the 1930s. Smiths was one of the first firms to move to the Great West Road, opening a single storey factory in 1927. They proved so successful that in 1930 they built a much larger factory with an impressive colonnaded front.

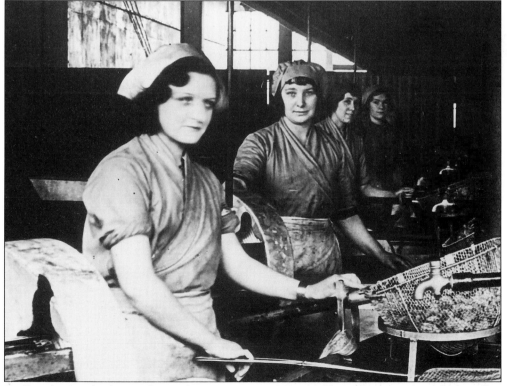

Staff in the Smiths factory frying chip potatoes in 1959. Another interesting Brentford smell!

The Christmas lights along the Great West Road were well known in years past. They are seen here from the Firestone factory in 1965.

Six

Gunnersbury Park

Gunnersbury Park originally consisted of two separate estates each with fine houses and grounds. The large mansion with its extensive gardens was bought by the Rothschild family in 1835, in whose hands it remained for nearly a century. They added the small mansion and its grounds to their estate in 1889. Many glittering social events were held here and the family were also generous benefactors to local good causes. The estate came into public ownership in 1925: the large mansion now houses the local museum and the grounds form an extensive public park.

The garden front of the large mansion (properly named Gunnersbury Park) early this century with the rose beds trained into basket shapes. The house was built in about 1802 to replace an earlier house. The gardens were reputedly laid out by William Kent for the Princess Amelia, a previous owner; the Rothschilds were keen gardeners and made many improvements.

The terrace of the large mansion in 1902, with Leopold de Rothschild, who had become sole owner of the estate in 1901; he is seen here in his $6\frac{1}{2}$ horsepower Bardon. He also bred racehorses; his horses won the Derby in 1879 and 1904. The plants in tubs were a feature of the gardens.

Two of the staff in the mid-1890s:
Mrs Sarah Foster, a dairy maid, and
her daughter Mrs Keefe, standing
outside the North Lodge.

The Pink Saloon, formerly the drawing room of the large mansion, taken in the early years of
this century. This room now houses the museum's collection of carriages.

The small mansion, properly named Gunnersbury House, from a postcard of the 1930s. Although the two houses were built about the same time and are rather close together, they were separately owned until 1889 when the small mansion was bought by Leopold de Rothschild, thereby uniting the two estates.

The teams taking part in a charity cricket match in the grounds of Gunnersbury Park, on 11 September 1903, between the Leopold de Rothschild XI and the G.W. Beldam XI. Two members of the Rothschild team were members of the family – Evelyn Rothschild, seated in the front row, second from the left (he was killed in 1917) and his younger brother Anthony (died 1961). The match was for the benefit of Acton Cottage Hospital which benefited by the sum of seventy pounds.

The Round Pond in 1902, showing the early eighteenth century temple, said to have been used as a billiard room in the early nineteenth century.

Outside the north front of the large mansion, showing the tree-moving team in either 1920 or 1921. Mr Gilbert, one of the team, later reminisced that they 'were always tree shifting'.

Farm workers in Gunnersbury Park, said to be standing by the last haystack erected there in 1920, in the big field. Mr Swansel the foreman is the man in the bowler hat standing second from the left.

Wheat grown on the Rothschild estate in 1917.

The official party at the opening of the park to the public on 26 May 1926. In the centre is the Right Honourable Neville Chamberlain, then Minister of Health, and next to him is Alderman Miss Smee, who played a major role in establishing the museum which opened in the large mansion in 1929. The Mayor of Acton is standing in the back row and the Mayor of Ealing is sitting on the extreme right. After the death of Lionel de Rothschild in 1917, some of the land was sold for housing. Then in 1925, 186 acres and both mansions were jointly bought for £125,000 by the boroughs of Acton and Ealing with help from the Middlesex County Council. Brentford and Chiswick joined in the estate's ownership and management in 1927.

Three senior police officers keeping an eye on the prizes at the mounted police sports day, held in the park in 1926.

A horse and cart from the park's own work force, smartly turned out to take part in a horse show in Gunnersbury Park in 1927.